Garden

poems by Ellen Kline McLeod

ISBN 978-1-936373-21-5

Published in the United States by Unbound Content, LLC, Englewood, NJ.
Cover art: Tree ©2011, by Ellen Kline McLeod.
Author photo: Sofia Tata
The poems in this collection are all original and previously unpublished with the exception of those specifically credited as first published elsewhere.

Garden
poems by Ellen Kline McLeod
First edition 2011

To my mother, Grace Ellen Costlow,
grandmothers, Mildred Ann Betz Costlow and Mary Bell Santmyers Kline Cottrill,
and their mothers, Elva Helen White Betz and Ethel Beatrice Putnam Santmyers.

I am grateful especially to Amy Coquillard and Cassie Premo Steele who were present, holding my hands, breathing and writing with me as this baby's birth began.

Some journeys begin intentionally. Some occur accidentally. This book represents both. I certainly intended to write poetry from my experiences as a woman: mother, wife, sister, daughter, friend, writer. But while I was flinging words like milk chocolate dirt from earth up to the sky, watching life fall around me, I breathed the silty, salty smell and found new places in ancient story, a garden.

Stories of life's beginnings exist in many cultures. We are invited to imagine magnificent participants: the earth, the sun, a woman, stars, animals, a man, wind, sea—a wondrous start. What might these players do? What might they become? What is it about them that is us? What if a creation story was told from another perspective, perhaps the woman's? *Garden* is a creation story.

—Ellen Kline McLeod

Table of Contents

Introduction 7

Creation

Our Delegation..11
In the Beginning..12
Welcome to the Struggle 13
Voice 1: Preacher..14
Voice 2: Guardian...15
Voice 3: Stranger..16
The Not...17

Excommunication

Leaves..21
Drunk Me and He 22
Blues...24
The Rain..25
Woman Heeds the Tree 26

Birth

Transition..31
Watch Her Be Born...32
What I Lost 34
First Corinthians 13: The Mother Daughter Verses..................................36
To My Daughter 38
Always the Question: Where to Go..39

Woman

Shaman 43
To Be of Use 44
Mason Jars 46
Who Decides It...47

Truth

Go, Girl Dog...51
Envy of the Lesbian...52
The Wall..53
Come On 54
Dandelion Day...55
Perhaps the Dream 56

About the Author..59

Introduction: Entering the Garden of Everyday Mystery

In this book, you are being invited into a garden. It is a garden of myth and memory. It is a sacred garden. It is the garden we were banished from. It is the garden of our dreams. It is a garden of everyday mystery. And it has been in you, growing, all along.

Two years ago, a woman came to me. She said, *I want to write.* So weekly we sat in my Co-Creating Studio and we wrote together.

What impressed me about Ellen Kline McLeod from the very beginning was how deep she was willing to go.

How courageous she was in saying what so many women feel:
Calculated carpool minutes march past
never first and never last to meet the children,
praise their smarts
wave pat pack into horseless carts.

How strong her words came out:
Lost is the ability to think myself a single untangled entity without umbilical
separate from this child and those who will appear after her.

How she does not hide from the truth of pain:
She did not lie and tell me everything would be easy
only pain does ease.

How unbreakable her vision of how we might re-enter that garden:
I will cry water over the earth for new growth green sprouts among decay.

In your aloneness, reader, take down this book from the shelf. Hold it to yourself. Begin to enter. Go beyond that fence. Find the garden. It is here.
The green growing place in which dreams plant abundant
offerings: food, desire.

One woman went into herself one day and did not shy away from what she found there. It was a garden. It was growing. It was abundant. There were other women there. There was more than enough to share.
Just as the sun and moon
call always to each other, come on.
And they do. So can you.

—Cassie Premo Steele

Creation

Our Delegation

Three people are a delegation:
>Triangulated strength to see all sides.
Protect one in the middle if she is weak or worry-wandered.
Dance a circle of joy.
Fetch wine, make bread, ready the table.
A delegation's united mission:
>Be the We the world cannot thrive without.
Three women are God.

In the Beginning

Spinning top with colors whirling, child's toy.
deity dainty tot-hand pinching the head between fingers to twirl
round and round with dizzying speed and no control
but a pattern, a course, an ultimate place
making beauty
in the air
on the ground
circling path twirling tribal dancer

Energy generated in motion runs the lights.
ten-tipped turbines twisting under flowing thought as writing hands
orbiting and illuminating the earth unknown with pulses
of inspiration and potential and space
powering insight
and purpose
with fire currents
burning center of the good dance

Swimming body struggle or float, conductor.
lapping lakes of life days ticked off as lived, anticipate those to come
stroke after stroke with kicks propel toward a shore of peace
and rest and memory of the race
speeding forward
relentless progress
waves of joy and sadness
carrying tenderly us the unstoppable circle

Welcome to the Struggle

God called. It's your first day. New clothes? no way—you'll go in naked. Squish and scream into skin, find books from living dying kin Aramaic parables enthrall with power to connect, shackle in shame, cower. Preaching you deserve not creation given your sinful state. Breathe, pant, fight through fatigue, do not wear out if it grows late. Much wisdom mixed with words may overpower soft voices. Life without doubt looms gray good and evil choices. God does not banish himself but stretches each arm a vine toward that outside the box of time, sacred succession of days precious if not fair. Plod pilgrim, debating about winning or losing, your singing soul will find no satisfaction choosing any destination but moving from God in God toward God. Blisters on the end of your tongue from storytelling, knots in your knuckles weaving and wares selling. Body time brings despair. What you require rests in beginnings bare. Welcome to the Struggle.

Voice 1: Preacher

I don't know what is where the voice is not.
The voice tells me I cannot do
without him I am worthless and weak
The preacher prescribes persevere
Don't let that weak babble come out of your mouth ever again.
Don't eat that; exercise; shave your legs; drop ten pounds
Why can't you just do it?
Where is your will?
Hail other Marys who do it all full of grace
world without
endless decent dinners healthy, economical, organic, quick
satisfying to everyone in the family
What is wrong with you?
Now and at the hour of death
Do you hear me?

Voice 2: Guardian

Why does it have to make me so tired
my voice companion
The audible attendant keeps me
moving otherwise I might succumb
to the guillotine
for lack of the one true faith.
I cannot evict the voice
inside cells without windows
wishing for summer's beaches where
I try not caring for a while.
Is it feasible not to ponder passed
love that rips heartflesh scraping
barbed wire as sounds try to escape
inquiring if the voice is an advocate?
No one else is talking

Voice 3: Stranger

Do I hear strange voices?
My head voice resides resonant from me, nothing strange.
One, not many, and it is my own or maybe God's
multi-layered polysyllabic prose-pillowed
voice proclaiming
do more faster correctly with vision and authenticity
don't be a faker, a fraud.
Yells and cries echo
now I lay me not to waste nor to err nor pick wrongly
may angels guard me not to break down and not to stop and get some rest
the servant-sergeant never ceases except in sleep
exhaustion's purple envelope hides me and crying drowns the virulent
voice proclaiming
don't be a baby, a blubberer.
I will cry water over the earth for new growth green sprouts among decay.
The voice relents, cry if you must but not for long.
Not for long.

The Not

Paralyzed panic
pick out what not to do
and in choosing the not
hang from it for eternity.

Dizzy
Dangling
Swaying pendulum unable to articulate what to want:
        not disorder—books plans puzzles standing shelf erect
        not disharmony—siblings arranged content dreaming

What not to do leads
instead of choosing
persisting purely the constant
not choosing
not knowing
not being
not chasing
mouth or legs cannot chase
as a sun-rotted clothesline
having slithered up from below
entwined ankles, knees, thighs
constricted heaving heart and lungs
pulling arms to body tingly tight
enslaving rope burned neck
gagging tearing kissing lip flesh
knotted tongue tastes blood and is sanctified.

Excommunication

Leaves .

Leaves litter the path home, lingering silhouettes
some colored imprints of decaying veins and skin
pounded by rain and sun into one with the ground
up companions remain on trees yet to be stripped
by breeze and time will take them eventually as
days of growing are gone and the moment to fall
arrives as gnarled knuckles of brown and yellow
blow among ruddy roots liberated to pile together
soon all the branches bare themselves to heaven
for the waiting after the green, the gold, the red
comes dead of winter when sap is still and deep
hidden until the season arrives to leave again.

First appeared at vox poetica, *October 2011*

Drunk Me and He

I am drunk and
I love it but cannot
share it because he
is asleep he
is asleep he
doesn't know me
anyway he
is cheerless and alone he
could share happy me
if he just opened out to feel
what I can be but he
does not and me
too drunk to think clearly
Except that I wish he
would welcome me.

If he would reach for me
I would climb like a vine
up a trellis toward
the sun but he
will not let me be
part of what holds him up he
is too sad he
is too sad me
I am not sad and

Garden

that makes him angry he
is too angry he
is too angry me
I am not angry
And that makes him resentful
I am not resentful he
sleeps dreaming fitful
dreams of misery he
is not prepared for me.

Blues

Hue of tears and
dingy denim and his
eyes that don't see
me anymore
the sky (higher mommy).
Reflections puddle soft
fleece blanket wrapped
sleeping lap baby breath is
the only life.

Sobbing subsided fuzzy
glass slipper feet pad
toward kitchen
evening's flicker
quietly.
Sheets shirts, pants pajamas
mind hands and flop
into pestilent piles
thought heaps without joy.

The Rain

Where is the green growing place in which dreams plant abundant offerings: food, desire. Tomatoes ripe red or possibly pomegranates fat with scarlet seeds that tempt Persephone tied to the underworld with a mate to whom much has been promised within whose ebony root cellar sprawl permanently entangled shoots in shared soil after pollination rise sprigs of new life. Figs feel more compelling than apples. Figs should have been the forbidden fruit trickling from woman's hunger dropping seeds into grass amid flowers. Tulips budding hot fuchsia array guarding purple white turnips forming unseen beside squash and eggplant and beans, sensible vegetables of lesser temptation but also in need of water. As for the rain no one knows if it will come or not.

Woman Heeds the Tree*

Garden grassland grown seeds not by humans sown
seated she in trickled tangerine haze
flickery winking maple leaves gaze
black-bound book open, weighty
God's word.

Grand golden tree beckons blessed woman see
endless eyes, prayer dances and rain
leaves dropped soon sprouted again
upon your heart and unto your children
God's law.

Rise love as once before creation covenant restore
who more surprised than she
summoned by a hardwood tree
inquires about a song for the people
God's promise.

Grassy blades to see rise, even slug elevates its eyes
wood embraced sings notes three
do not be afraid but attend to me
the tree chants ahavah
God's love.

Wings wait feeling deep languid liquid tranquility seep
branches long to light, roots in soil
upward growth from heritage uncoil
voices wilderness wandered cry—love
God's presence.

Garden

Humanity's reminder song passes steady stillness long
then butterfly breeze blows once more
pollen and insects scurry as before
into rites time's patient passage breath
God's mystery.

Arms from tree return to book standing final look
carrying a dance, a chant, a sway
each upon the song sent our way
pounding heart beat drums and fugue fury
God's call.

Abundant creation is not free destroy it and kill me
and you and him and her and all
Hear the horns sound the call
we do not survive if we sever stretched limbs of creation
God's wrath.

If the composer hears the tree why not you, why not me
seated in symphonic supplication found
chorus and tympani rise from ground
roots searching down, limbs longing rising up
God's children.

Majestic mountains for our view the sky's changing hue
freely given and taken if we
heed not the wizened tree
a sick mother cannot make milk and all will starve without
God's garden.

*Inspired by Meira Warshauer's Ahavah from her CD, Streams in the Desert

Birth

Transition

The birthing book displays diagrams and detailed facts
figures sprawled supported by science but no one
certainly no chap can
ever explain transition: the time from eight to ten
nothing hurts more
than the final fearful frantic phase of opening
oneself to expose
unknown life.

Watch Her Be Born

She may be headed for a C.
Prep the mother.
Monitor the baby.

Faces gaze upon paper
white patient perched
on a table top trapeze

When spotlight shines
and music blares
everyone will see

inside and know
words rave in her body.
Mercury maid

thoughts gauge
toxic tolerance levels
letting inner expression

drip potential poison
slowly into veins.
A mother body

can handle much
and survive. Words
fly over eyes.

Garden

Blood smears paper
making a spectacle.
Shimmering swing

without a safety net
swift syllabic silhouette.
No figure can cry

blood they'll say.
A screaming sticky
faced child waves

circus streamers
Beyond taut tent top
death defying feats

dangling from a
strong white cord.
Scrambling to lift

sequined lines
out of the womb
hovering above

the earth recording
what goes on there.
Watch her be born.

What I Lost

Dear St. Anthony please come around. Something's been lost and cannot be found.

The moment is dark. Night fallen and dawn an elusive promise yet to be fulfilled.
Sheets sterile white bear the only thing like light. Illumination a notion inside thought.
I feel self-conscious because I am screaming but sister says it was a whimper.
My earsplitting mind decides to push her out.
Acknowledged.

Lost virginity is confirmed. Fear is consuming us and the crown appears.
Sweat suggests past labor left behind never to be forgotten.
I recoil into myself to call the women I have been for their cumulative strength.
Welcome another banished child of Eve.
Expelled.

She emerges strong, angry, screaming. Sister says this surely was screaming.
Demanding her day in the sun out of the darkness where she has grown.
I see beauty unmatched swaddled in a heated blanket eyes wide unfocused.
The child, my first daughter, begins.
Loved.

Fissures are cleaned and stitched. She seeks me, my warmth and sustenance.
As the tiny being nurses I am all she needs. I think this is enough.
At her birth I trust the power of good and love and motherhood. Her soul within her
from within me so proud to have made her and brought her here.
Nourished.

Garden

.

The room's lights impostor the sun. No windows here (but no one sees this).
She and I do not allow that my milk will dry and my arms will fail to protect her.
I do not think of what is lost. What she may lose. Consumed with what I have made
I see it is good as beginning God-life from chaos which also had ahead a rocky time.
Created.

Lost is the ability to think myself a single untangled entity without umbilical
separate from this child and those who appear after her from my womb into light.
Left in the sheets are prints of fuller thighs and feelings larger than my youth.
Lost is the grab my purse and dash day traded for knapsack, rations, and stroller.
Prepared.

Lost is keeping my life all my own as I would gladly give it for this child.
Lost is freedom of my mind and body. Not completely mine any more
but shared and relentless in my drive to tend and protect the person I hold.
Lost, too, weakness and inability; endurance is the only option allowed.
Survived.

First Corinthians 13: The Mother Daughter Verses

My blood began at a party I never wanted to attend.
I should have known—cramps, moodiness, aching back.
Tears trickled down my cheeks horrified hiding crimson panty stain.
Mom led to the bathroom armed with supplies, then my room.
From her bed gathered down cover, wrapping fat blue-grey paisley around my body.
>   *Sometimes keeping extra warm helps ease the cramps*, she said.
She did not lie and tell me everything would be easy
only pain does ease.
She did not make me talk
but lay me to rest in a small corner room with great-grandmother's blue-light lamp.
>   My daughter flicks the blue lamp's switch now by her bed where we read.
>   I remember puffy quilt eaten by time's teeth and imagine future
>   first day of her period can be beautiful.
Mothers believe all things.

My first crush was so deep I assumed I would never love again.
I should have known—not calling, avoiding, turned back.
Blue mascara smeared face watched pretty prom blond kiss.
Mother prayed I would not choose him young listened unnoticed as I told a friend.
>   *You are too young to commit yourself—just have a good time*, she said.
She did not lie and tell me everything would be easy
only pain does ease.
She did tell me to try again
but avoid boys get out of town find my own apartment with my own room just for me.
>   My daughter cries because she has a boy project partner and her classmates tease.
>   I wonder why kids are so mean. She says she does not want a boyfriend
>   for a long time. I am glad.
Mothers hope all things.

Garden

My voice declared the dove descended at my confirmation.
I should have known—Word, work, prostrate back.
Mom perched in the pew perhaps pride perhaps fury remembering choices.
> *Pray for guidance but remember to think for yourself, too,* she said.
She did not lie and tell me everything would be easy
only that pain does ease.
She did not tell me she lost her voice reading scripture
years after sitting in a closet brown confessional telling youthful sins sharing his room.
> My daughter looks at a wedding to see if I cross kneel stand.
> I long to languish in this ritual imbued into the fabric of my soul
> but I cannot ingest all they preach.
Mothers endure all things.

My baby was born in dark dawn after twelve hours waiting.
I should have known—bulbous belly, pushing, arching back.
My mother home perhaps remembering birth waiting for my call.
> *Having your mother at the birth is not necessarily a good thing,* she said.
She did not lie and tell me everything would be easy
only pain does ease.
She did not say aloud that baby me unplanned and fast
laid out a layette of unopened dreams from a room shared with sisters.
> My daughter announces she does not want to have a baby.
> I realize repulsion to brown-lined basketball body vagina exit
> but secretly hope she will change her mind.
Mothers bear all things.

Love never failed faltered perhaps guessed wrong but when I was a child I never doubted.
Mother mirror flesh heart skin bone I cannot know fully as I am fully unknown.
Words spoken and unsaid gave me a map, pray like she to be the greatest of these.

First appeared at Literary Mama, *November 2009*

To My Daughter

First I
was a daughter playing
with dolls and strollers.
Then I grew
you: real.
Not playing anymore I loved
you so much
I thought I might pop.

Always the Question: Where to Go

Do leaves wonder where they want
to go, faces held toward the sun
palms open to morning rising
candy sweet on the tongue, yellow
sugar light showing the direction
east: beginning to know life
and only one distinct direction of up

Woman

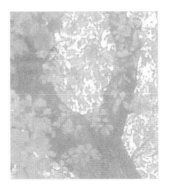

Shaman

Shaman woman poet wise possesses clear seeing water-sky eyes
breathing journal dance with pen
hold my hand when I begin
stepping out
breaking down
growing fire.
Reaching graphite threads—grasping hold
knuckles bloodless squeezing cold
coal-black inklings across white page
butter beauty birth, magenta rage
silent not sound nor audible still
until parchment seduces quill.

Temple priestess of Mary's womb beckons play in sun scented room
real sometimes cannot be seen
without risk of coming clean
of lies
told by us
to ourselves
because pretense is
of use to us.
Fear of unmasking rumbles rhythm chance
heart pounding wild word romance
meaning may ascend from twisted line
alphabet ink-map of a tousled mind.

To Be of Use

Lead body mornings fall in line
up I rise before the shine of dawn to wake the babies,
make the gruel
dress cuddle kiss goodbye to school.

Strong arm laundry shirts and pants
mounds and heaps stained knee dance to clean the darks,
sparkle white
dry fold closet away tuck tight.

Grocery gallop before high noon
toddler happy school ends soon to peanut butter lunch,
dirty dishes
chew swallow fulfill coffee wishes.

Calculated carpool minutes march past
never first and never last to meet the children,
praise their smarts
wave pat pack into horseless carts.

Snack sucked down without chewing
reluctant homework help doing to push achievement,
upon my shoulder
math spelling journal back in the folder.

Garden

Practice piano time tempo tapping
dress for karate energy lapping to arrive on time,
toddler's wail
kids bags purse phone, check the mail

Worker ants finally file home
balance dinner talking on the phone to plan soccer,
library volunteer
calendar checked magnetically near.

Bath time with soapy splashing
clean towels and pajamas dashing with lotion in tow,
books read
tomorrow's list prepared and welcoming bed.

Mason Jars

wonder filled inheritance
from grandmother's pantry in her
one room homestead expanded as chance
cycles passed and children came

jars packed pickles' zing
butter beans, tomatoes, first fruits
from hopeful sunny seeded spring
sweet blackberry preserves and pepper relish

summer presented fresh-picked food
abundant from the sandy garden
jars offered stashed moonshine merry mood
or cool cascading sugary tea

filled, emptied unbroken pass
offering for family feasts or famine
endless value strong vase of reusable glass
These jars can hold anything.

Who Decides It

Who your mother is decides it
not only because of what she feeds
you for nine months but where she is
from, who she chooses to become
the city in which she dwells does
not create your cells but may do more
than DNA to determine what choices
you get whether or not you end up in
doing time for crime that chose you
before you were born to people who were
born to people who thought they might
make it out of the womb that holds them
until they escape the beginnings and run
run out of town without tripping
dripping blood and fluid and a trail
of syringes or snorted lines drawn before life
even began by the boundaries of town
the city or planet every person happens
to inhabit shapes it as colorful playdoh
pride and loyalty and an end to it all
dawn arrives over sirens and the sleeping
street speckled cobblestones and broken
glass cradling tumbled down drunks
who themselves just born around the corner
haven't fallen far from home.

Truth

Go, Girl Dog

The bitch ain't bad b'ness
in the news by dancing
drunk with praise and love
as long as she doesn't give
herself away she can grind
her love over any dessert
she chooses to groove in
her club or with her cubs
when the music plays she
will dance and doesn't give
a damn what anybody thinks

Envy of the Lesbian

Although the body is not the soul
can tell which have want to join and
she is beautiful, laughter and pure
dancing honesty about who she is
and loves and raises and though she
is spectacular, I do not want her
body beyond the beauty of a sister,
friendship having found it is not my
disposition but to be her even amid
senseless struggle in society that
doesn't appreciate that she is and
has a wife, loving mother sharing her
life journey and at night's end to
hear her name spoken by thoughtful
female mouth even though I do not
want to kiss is a gift I wish was mine

The Wall

Wall in for safety and to keep the lawn
well tended and brutish beasties out.
But wonder what creature might be
held in, what unkempt wheat or vines
hang about undiscovered within? Dig
a hole, gnaw an opening, perhaps
first poke a peephole to peer out
for spies, enemies, cohorts. Perchance
pull your carcass over just to see if
you can. First your right leg then
the left to fling flop the fence.
Flattened on your back, look up
eyes squint in the sun sprinkled through
applauding leaves; no one sees but
sniggering trees and they're not telling.
Look back, see the wall crumble
vastness becomes you watched over
and not, everything grew. Young you knew
world without end, why did you forget

Come On

a moment changes everything
—David Gray

Who is calling, come on, come on
Not a past self, it's my tomorrow
self and I do not know her but a
moment changes everything she
knows I believe anything is possible
except to keep time still the night
always comes and day follows. Just
as the sun and moon call always to
each other, come on. And they do.
So can you. Speak the truth always
with kindness and forethought.
Come on.

Dandelion Day

Dailiness as dandelions who
sprout yellow petals to puff
fluffy white and float when
we do not know but to be
saffron today in God's palm
without fear of what being
lifted into the air to plant
elsewhere might feel like
the present butter-hued being
one new day open golden
the exact life we have already

Perhaps the Dream

Perhaps
The dream is
wanting to know tomorrow (who we could become).
Remember
project
a prophetic proposal
trusting that where we have been is valuable.

The cycle has knowledge
we cannot articulate (without dance and drumming).
To realize what
to want
is a gift
moving
beyond safety to feeling the wish.

Perhaps
The dream is
to love
whatever we grow to be (birth without end).
Evolving vital
cause effect
expanding with each encounter.

Garden

The mission summons!
Send those made (our image and likeness)
more memory words
so each dream
stronger
embracing shoulders
who aspire to wanting forward together.

Ellen Kline McLeod lives in South Carolina with her husband and three children. She holds degrees from the University of Georgia's Grady College of

Journalism and Mass Communication and Loyola University Maryland's Graduate School of Education. She stirs together a childhood in rural Georgia, past careers in advertising and teaching middle school, marriage, motherhood, and a deep love of words to cook up poetry, short stories, and an under-construction novel. Ellen's work is published at *Literary Mama, vox poetica,* and *Referential Magazine* (all available online). She blogs weekly word reflections at MusingMondayMorning.blogspot.com.

10392038R00034

Made in the USA
Charleston, SC
01 December 2011